MW00604420

SAMUEL DE CHAMPLAIN

**Father of the New France | Exploration of the Americas
Biography 3rd Grade | Children's Biographies**

DISSECTED LIVES

DISSECTED LIVES
auto biographies

First Edition, 2019

Published in the United States by Speedy Publishing LLC, 40 E Main Street, Newark, Delaware 19711 USA.

© 2019 Dissected Lives Books, an imprint of Speedy Publishing LLC

All rights reserved.

Without limiting the rights under the copyright reserved above, no part of this publication may be reproduced, stored in or introduced into a retrieval system, or transmitted, in any form, or by any means (electronic, mechanical, photocopying, recording, or otherwise), without the prior written permission of the copyright owner.

All images in this book have been reproduced with the knowledge and prior consent of the artists concerned, and no responsibility is accepted by producer, publisher, or printer for any infringement of copyright or otherwise arising from the contents of this publication.

Dissected Lives Books are available at special discounts when purchased in bulk for industrial and sales-promotional use. For details contact our Special Sales Team at Speedy Publishing LLC, 40 E Main Street, Newark, Delaware 19711 USA. Telephone (888) 248-4521 Fax: (210) 519-4043. www.speedybookstore.com

10 9 8 7 6 * 5 4 3 2 1

Print Edition: 9781541950740
Digital Edition: 9781541952546

See the world in pictures. Build your knowledge in style.
https://www.speedypublishing.com/

TABLE OF CONTENTS

The Son of a Sea Captain...6

New France...10

Champlain in the New World...15

Champlain's 1604 Expedition..20

A Brutal Winter..25

Champlain's Exploration Continues......................................29

Two More Winters in Acadia...35

Champlain and the Discovery of Lakes...................................39

Champlain Establishes Quebec City......................................46

A Return to Exploring..49

Back in France...53

A Declining Colony...56

The Siege of Quebec City...59

Conclusion...64

Samuel de Champlain, a French explorer to the New World in the 1600s, helped to build permanent French settlements in what is now Canada, helped map the rivers, lakes, and coastlines of the region, and helped establish trade with the Native American tribes. Because Champlain laid the groundwork with his expeditions, French settlers were encouraged to colonize the New World. When he consolidated these colonies, Champlain earned the nickname, the Father of New France. Let's look at the life and legacy of this intrepid explorer.

Samuel de Champlain statue in front of the Chateau Frontenac in Quebec City, Canada

THE SON OF A SEA CAPTAIN

Samuel De Champlain

Samuel de Champlain was the son of a sea captain. Born in the tiny French port city of Brouage in 1567, Champlain learned all about sailing and navigating from his father. Being a good navigator was just as important as being a good sailor in those days because it meant they could return home again after their voyage was complete.

Samuel de Champlain

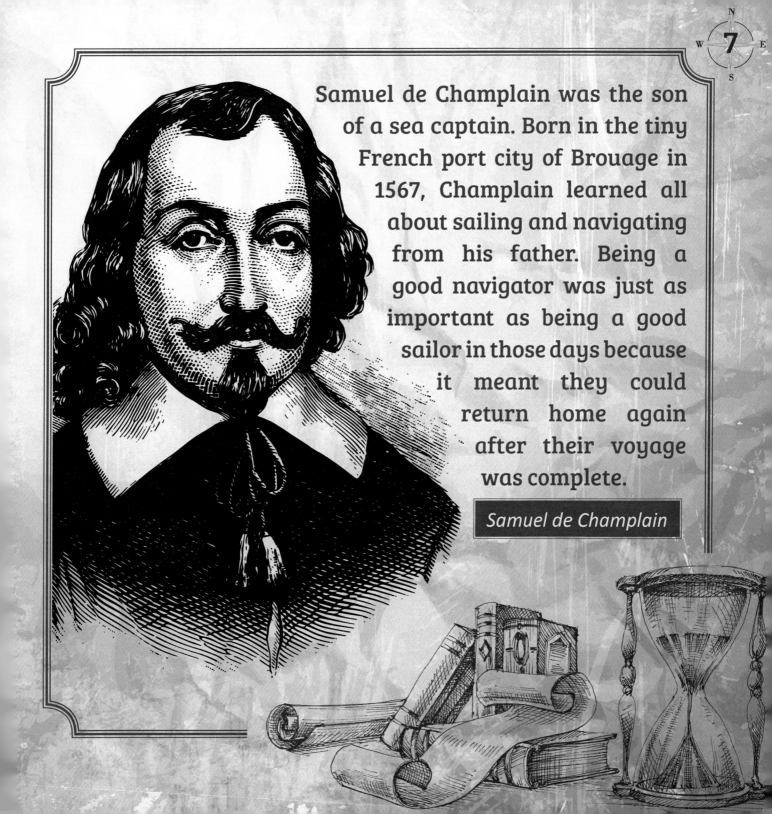

As a young man, Champlain proved his navigation skills by leading expeditions to Central America and the islands of the West Indies in the New World.

King Henry IV was pleased with Champlain's abilities and bestowed on him the honorary title of Royal Geographer. When planning began to build French settlements and trading posts in the area of the New World known as New France, the King gave the job to Samuel de Champlain.

King Henry IV of France

NEW FRANCE

Samuel De Champlain

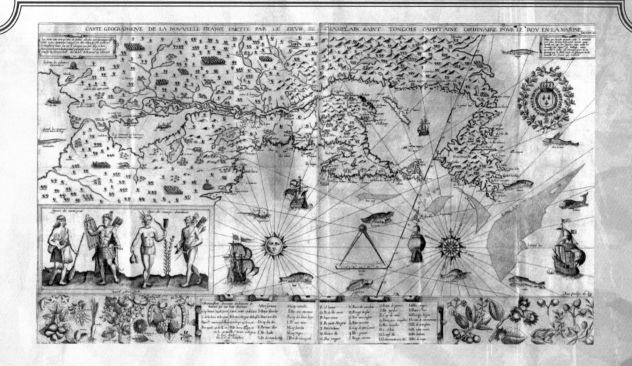

CARTE GEOGRAPHIQVE DE LA NOVVELLE FRANSE FAICTE PAR LE SIEVR DE CHAMPLAIN SAINT TONGOIS CAPPITAINE ORDINAIRE POVR LE ROY EN LA MARINE

Portions of Samuel de Champlain's first detailed map of New France, published in 1613, were created with the help of First Nations people.

For almost 250 years, the area extending from the eastern seaboard of Canada, along both shores of the Saint Lawrence River, into the eastern Great Lakes was known as New France.

From the time that Jacques Cartier first explored the Saint Lawrence River in 1534 until the region was ceded to the English and Spanish in 1763, French explorers, traders, and settlers flocked to the New World land for the rich natural resources found there.

A memoir of Jacques Cartier, his voyages to St. Lawrence

Jacques Cartier

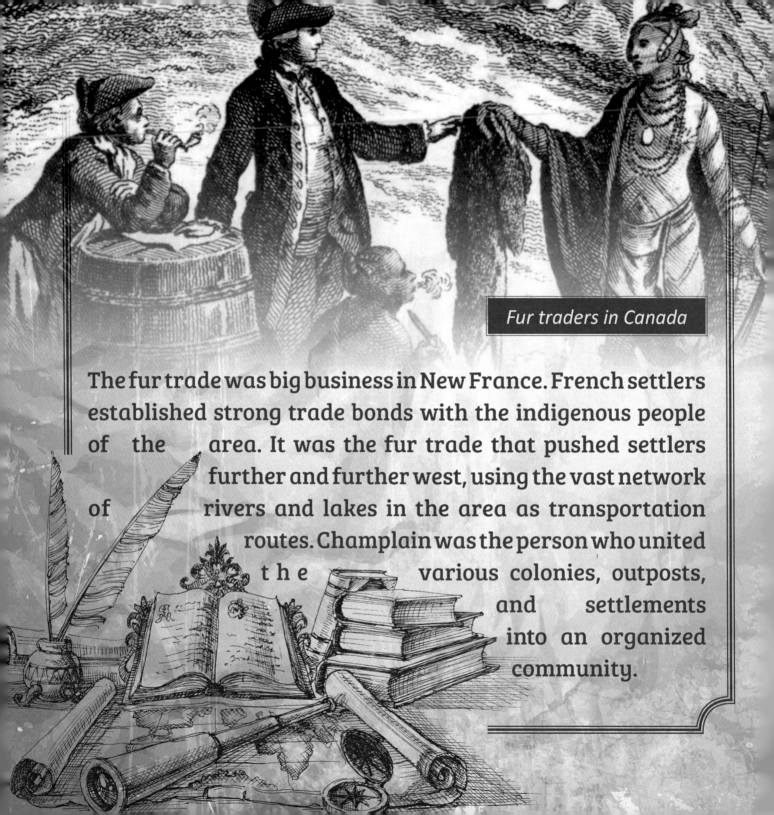

Fur traders in Canada

The fur trade was big business in New France. French settlers established strong trade bonds with the indigenous people of the area. It was the fur trade that pushed settlers further and further west, using the vast network of rivers and lakes in the area as transportation routes. Champlain was the person who united the various colonies, outposts, and settlements into an organized community.

CHAMPLAIN IN THE NEW WORLD

Samuel De Champlain

In 1603, Samuel de Champlain was invited by King Henry IV to join an exhibition led by Francois Grave Du Pont to the Saint Lawrence River, which was then call the River of Canada.

François Gravé Du Pont

Bridge across a river, Saint Lawrence River, Quebec, Canada

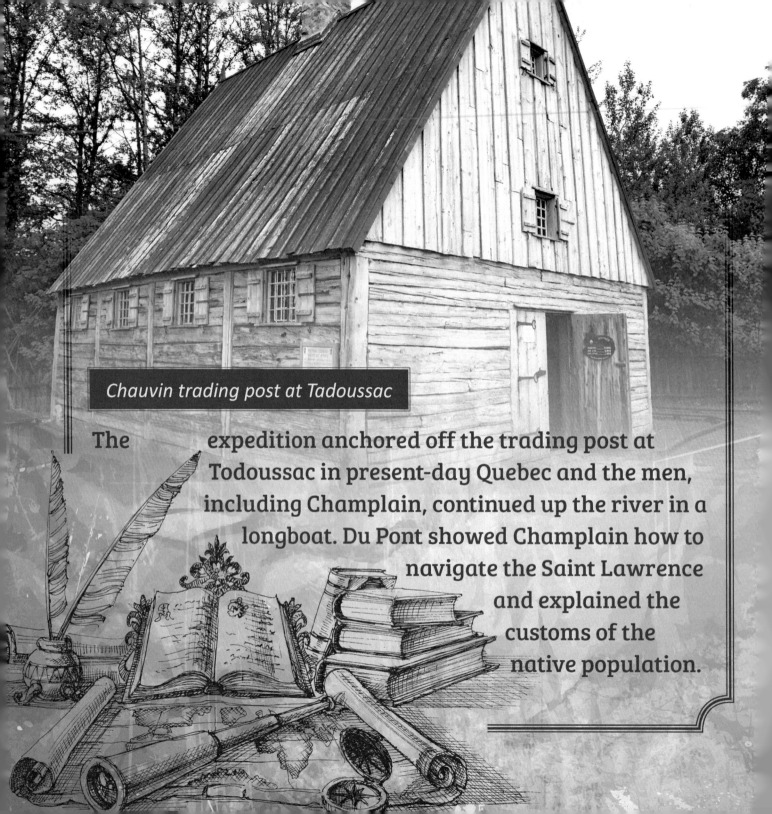

Chauvin trading post at Tadoussac

The expedition anchored off the trading post at Todoussac in present-day Quebec and the men, including Champlain, continued up the river in a longboat. Du Pont showed Champlain how to navigate the Saint Lawrence and explained the customs of the native population.

They landed at the site where the city of Montreal is now, prohibited from going further because of rapids. For this trip, Champlain's first visit to New France, he served primarily as an observer. He took detailed notes of his surroundings, and of the flora and fauna of the region. Back in France, Champlain's report of the area was published.

Champlain's representation in a boat with two Indians, descending from the rapids

CHAMPLAIN'S 1604 EXPEDITION

Samuel De Champlain

Monument of Pierre Du Gua de Monts, built in 2007 on Saint-Denis Avenue, near the Citadelle de Québec

The report that Samuel de Champlain presented to King Henry IV was so well-received that the king wanted to learn more about the New France region. He asked Champlain to go on a second New World expedition in the spring of 1604. This journey, headed by a French nobleman and merchant named Pierre Dugua de Mons, ended up lasting several years and turned into a battle for survival.

Sea Caves at Bay of Fundy

As with his previous expedition, Champlain began at the mouth of the Saint Lawrence River. From there, he traveled through the region called Acadia and thoroughly explored the Bay of Fundy.

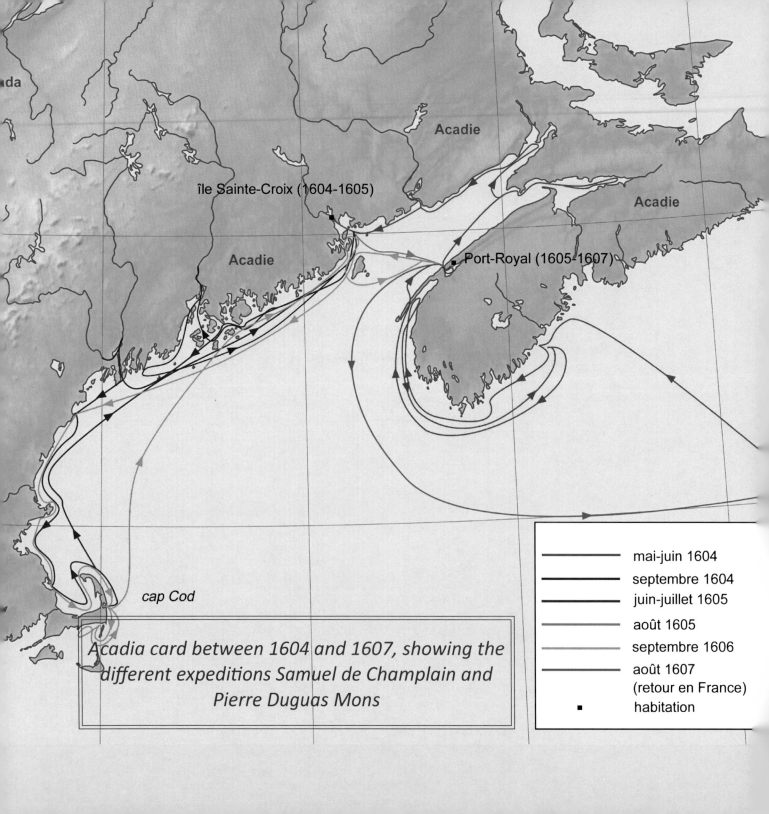

Acadie

île Sainte-Croix (1604-1605)

Acadie

Acadie

Port-Royal (1605-1607)

cap Cod

Acadia card between 1604 and 1607, showing the different expeditions Samuel de Champlain and Pierre Duguas Mons

	mai-juin 1604
	septembre 1604
	juin-juillet 1605
	août 1605
	septembre 1606
	août 1607 (retour en France)
■	habitation

A BRUTAL WINTER

Samuel De Champlain

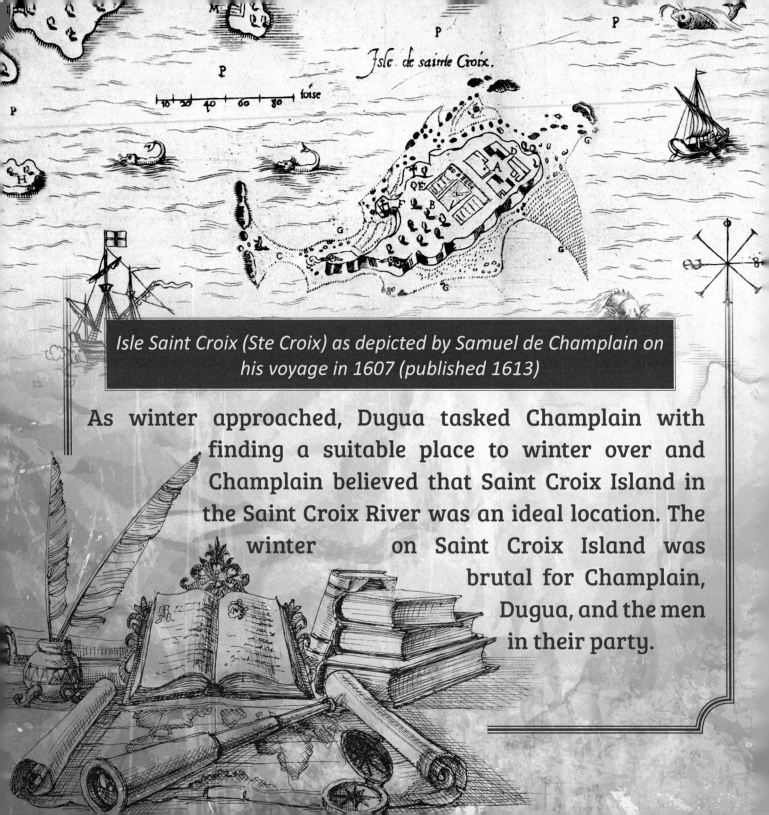

Isle Saint Croix (Ste Croix) as depicted by Samuel de Champlain on his voyage in 1607 (published 1613)

As winter approached, Dugua tasked Champlain with finding a suitable place to winter over and Champlain believed that Saint Croix Island in the Saint Croix River was an ideal location. The winter on Saint Croix Island was brutal for Champlain, Dugua, and the men in their party.

Saint Croix Island, as seen from the New Brunswick side of the St. Croix River

On top of the frigid conditions, the group suffered from the effects of scurvy, a painful and deadly disease caused by lack of vitamin C in one's diet. More than half of the members of the expedition died of scurvy that first winter.

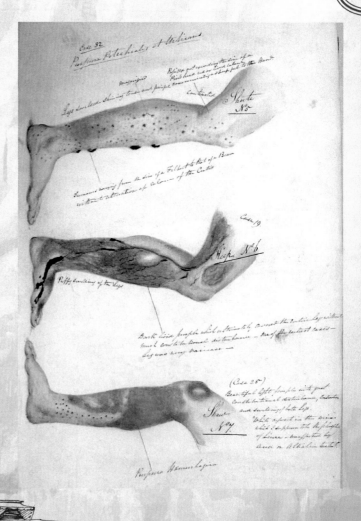

An illustration of Scurvy Case

CHAMPLAIN'S EXPLORATION CONTINUES

Samuel De Champlain

In the spring, they moved their settlement across the Bay of Fundy. Port Royal was constructed in early 1605. Port Royal is Canada's oldest settlement. Later renamed Annapolis by the British, this site served as Champlain's base of operations for the remainder of his expedition.

Port Royal National Historic Site in Port Royal, Nova Scotia, Canada

Port Royal, Nova Scotia, Canada

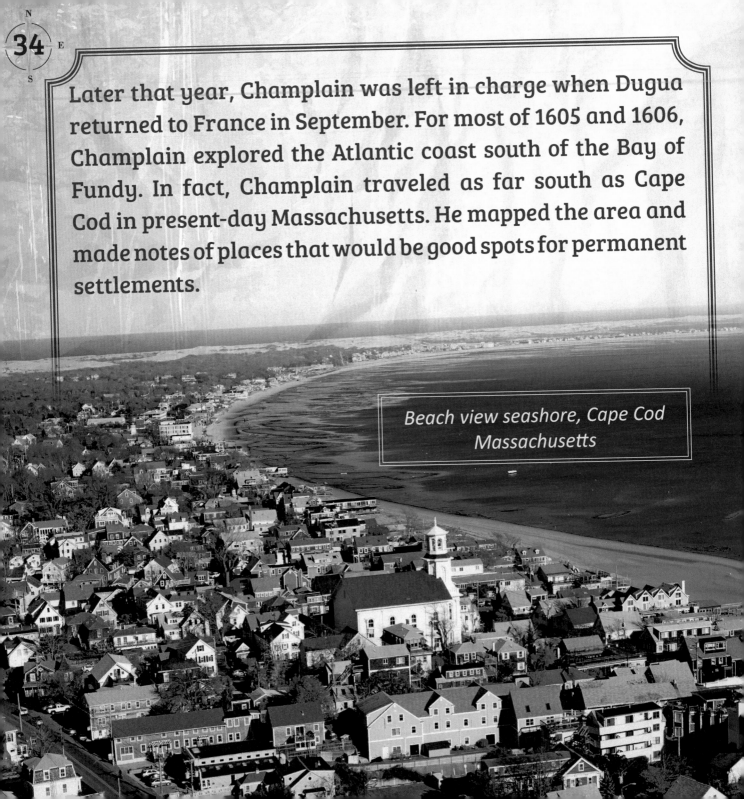

Later that year, Champlain was left in charge when Dugua returned to France in September. For most of 1605 and 1606, Champlain explored the Atlantic coast south of the Bay of Fundy. In fact, Champlain traveled as far south as Cape Cod in present-day Massachusetts. He mapped the area and made notes of places that would be good spots for permanent settlements.

Beach view seashore, Cape Cod Massachusetts

TWO MORE WINTERS IN ACADIA

Samuel De Champlain

Samuel de Champlain spent two more winters at the establishment of Port Royal and neither of these were as brutal or deadly as the first winter. When the weather was favorable, he explored and mapped the numerous bays, harbors, islands, inlets, and rivers of the region. He produced more detailed and accurate maps than his rivals, the English.

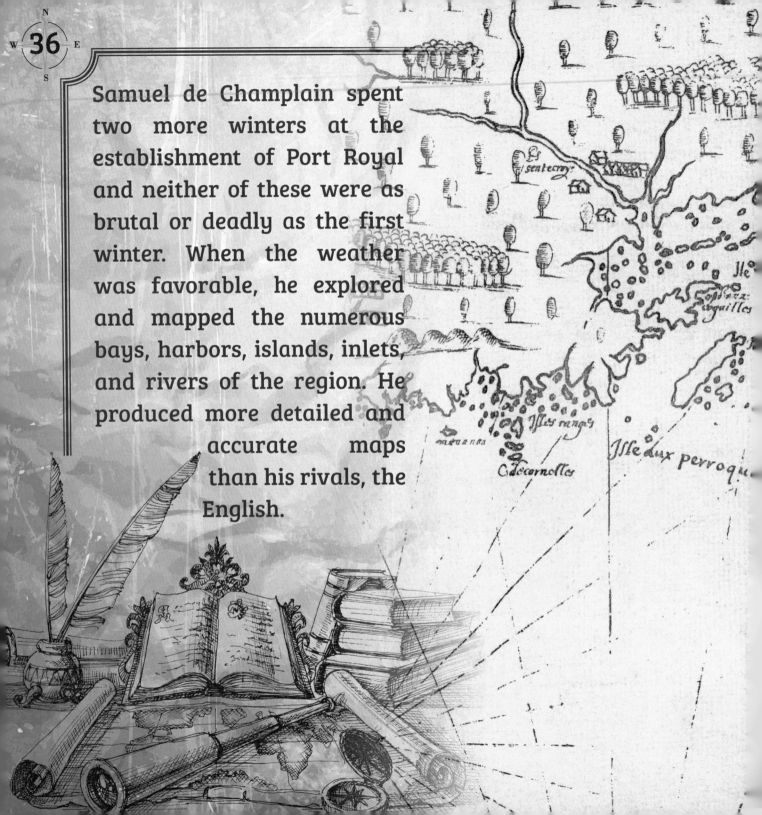

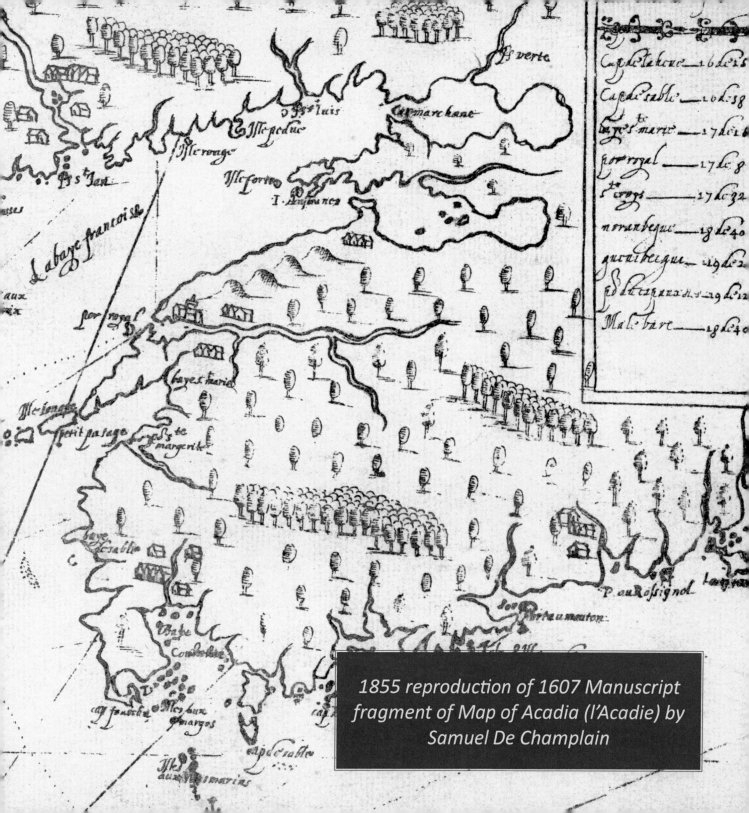

1855 reproduction of 1607 Manuscript fragment of Map of Acadia (l'Acadie) by Samuel De Champlain

In 1607, English settlers established a colony in the southern part of Acadia, near what is now Kennebec, Maine. Although this colony was abandoned after just one year, King Henry IV was concerned that the English may encroach on New France. It was time to increase the colonization of New France.

Augusta, Maine, USA downtown skyline on the Kennebec River.

CHAMPLAIN AND THE DISCOVERY OF LAKES

Samuel De Champlain

Later in his travels, Samuel de Champlain discovery two of the five Great Lakes, Lake Ontario and Lake Huron. Obviously, these massive bodies of freshwater were known to the native populations for centuries, but Champlain was the first European explorer to see these giant lakes, which are actually more like freshwater seas.

The beautiful Toronto's skyline over Lake Ontario

Lake Huron Shoreline in the Bruce Peninsula Shari Chambers

Champlain had befriended the Huron tribes and he joined them in a battle against their enemy, the Iroquois, in 1609. This battle took place in an area that is now part of the state of New York. It was there that he saw the lake that would eventually bear his name, Lake Champlain. This long, narrow body of water lies between the states of New York and Vermont and extended across the international border into Quebec.

Champlain's own illustration of his encounter with the Iroquois in July 1609

Champlain Bridge across Lake Champlain connecting New York and Vermont

CHAMPLAIN ESTABLISHES QUEBEC CITY

Samuel De Champlain

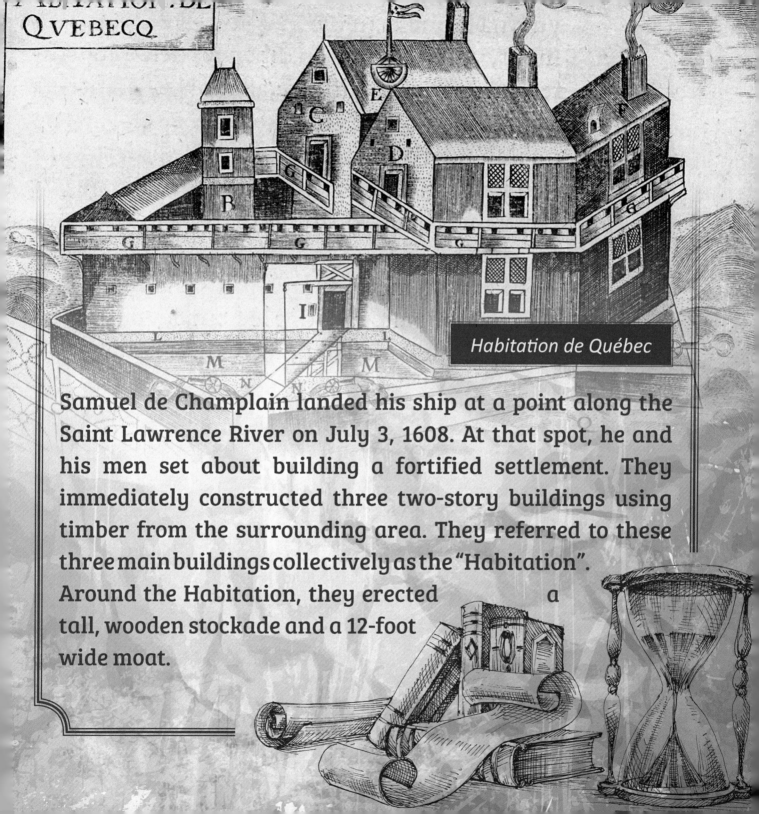

Habitation de Québec

Samuel de Champlain landed his ship at a point along the Saint Lawrence River on July 3, 1608. At that spot, he and his men set about building a fortified settlement. They immediately constructed three two-story buildings using timber from the surrounding area. They referred to these three main buildings collectively as the "Habitation". Around the Habitation, they erected a tall, wooden stockade and a 12-foot wide moat.

For the name of his new settlement, Champlain adopted the native Algonquian word, "kebec", which meant "place where the river narrows." He used a French spelling to give us the name "Quebec". Quebec City is one of the oldest European cities in all of North America.

Aerial view of Chateau Frontenac hotel and Old Port in Quebec City, Canada

A RETURN TO EXPLORING

Samuel De Champlain

With Quebec City firmly established, Samuel de Champlain resumed his exploration of New France. On May 27, 1613, he set out in search of a body of water that the Huron Indians called the "northern sea". They were most likely describing Hudson Bay.

His trek took him along the Ottawa River. In June of that year, Champlain had a meeting with the Algonquian chief, Tessouat, to establish an alliance. Although he was able to build relations with the native people and survey the land, Champlain did not find the northern sea t h a t he was looking for.

A Monument to the Algonquin Chief Tessouat in Ottawa

BACK IN FRANCE

Samuel De Champlain

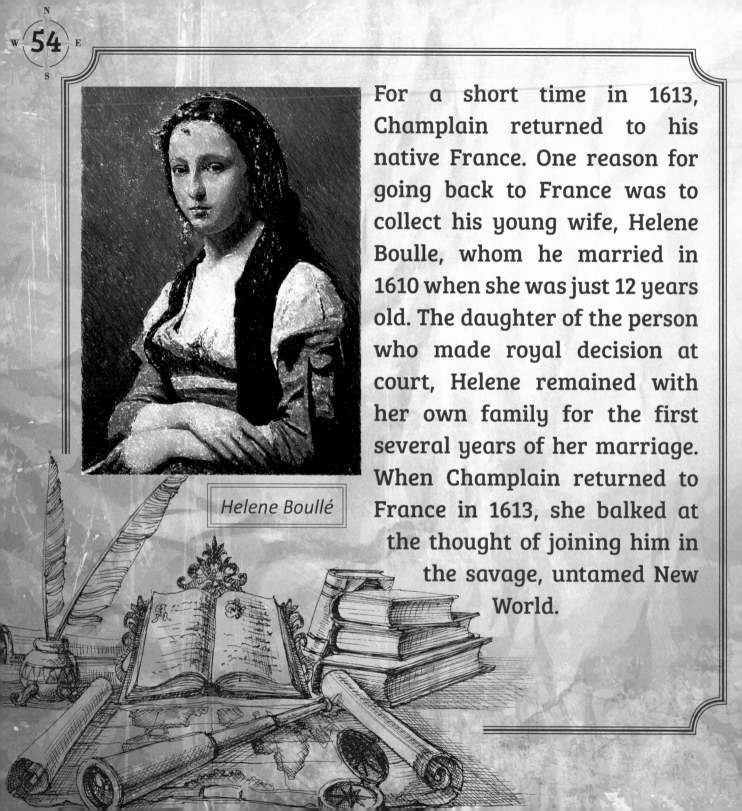

Helene Boullé

For a short time in 1613, Champlain returned to his native France. One reason for going back to France was to collect his young wife, Helene Boulle, whom he married in 1610 when she was just 12 years old. The daughter of the person who made royal decision at court, Helene remained with her own family for the first several years of her marriage. When Champlain returned to France in 1613, she balked at the thought of joining him in the savage, untamed New World.

She eventually did accompany her husband across the ocean and lived for several years in Quebec City. The other reason Champlain returned to France was so that he could publish the accounts of his explorations in New France. The King used Champlain's writings as a sales tool to encourage settlers to colonize New France. The more French settlers to the region, he knew, meant it was less likely that the English would take over the region.

Madame Champlain Teaching Indian Children

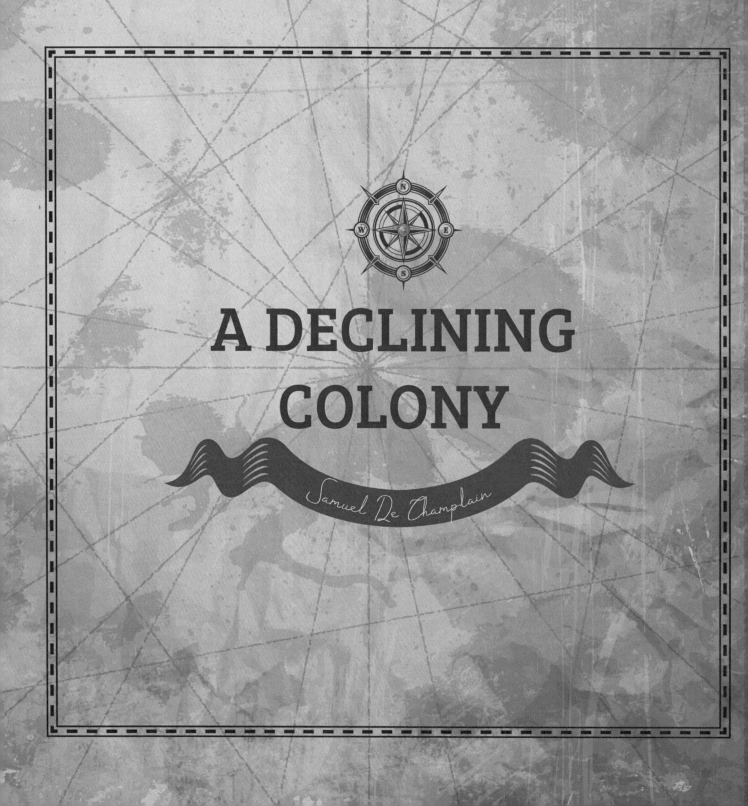

A DECLINING COLONY

Samuel De Champlain

Portrait of Louis XIII, King of France as a boy

The fur trading industry experiences an economic decline in 1611 and that hit New France hard. Many of the French sponsors of the colonies pulled their resources out of Quebec. Samuel de Champlain appealed to King Louis XIII to help keep the French settlements viable. In 1613, the King's viceroy appointed Champlain to the position of commandant of New France. Among his first order of business was to mend relations with the native population so that trade routes could be reestablished.

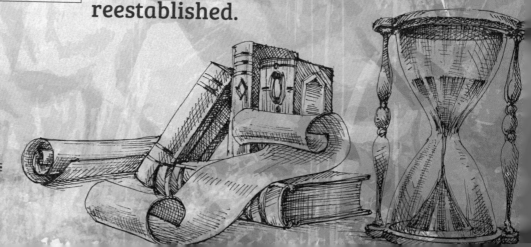

He brought together traders, trappers, and French missionaries to join him on his expeditions into the wilderness. By 1620, the French king had had enough of an absentee commandant. He reaffirmed Champlain's position as the leader of Quebec, but only after forbidding him for going on any more explorative treks. Instead, the king instructed him to stay in Quebec City to be an effective ruler.

Samuel de Champlain exploring the Canadian wilderness

THE SIEGE OF QUEBEC CITY

Samuel De Champlain

Under Champlain's leadership, however, the New France colony continued to flounder. The economy of the region was still heavily tied to the fur trade and settlers had not established large-scale farming operations or invested in other businesses. Still, the city of Quebec was a desirable target for the English.

Statue Champlain Nepean Point Ottawa

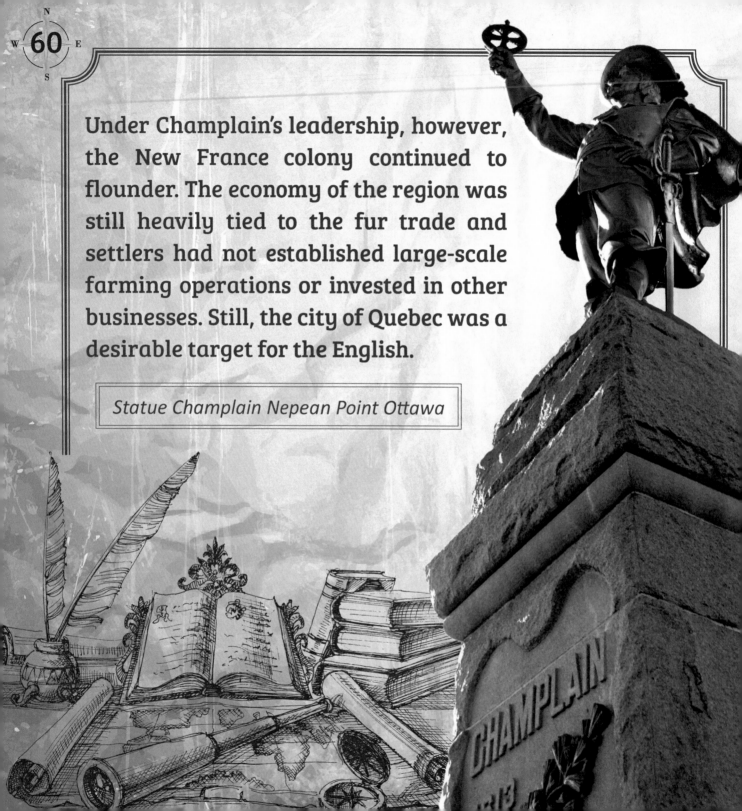

Champlain leaves Quebec as a prisoner aboard Kirke's ship

In 1628, the city was besieged by English privateers. Champlain and his men manned the defensive walls for several months until they ran out of food, gunpowder, and other supplies and were forced to surrender. Champlain was captured and sent to England as a prisoner until hostilities between the English and the French quieted down in 1632.

Champlain was released and returned to France where he wrote and published his seventh book about his exploits in the New World. He once again crossed the Atlantic to live in his beloved Quebec City. On Christmas day in 1635, Samuel de Champlain, the Father of New France, suffered a stroke and died.

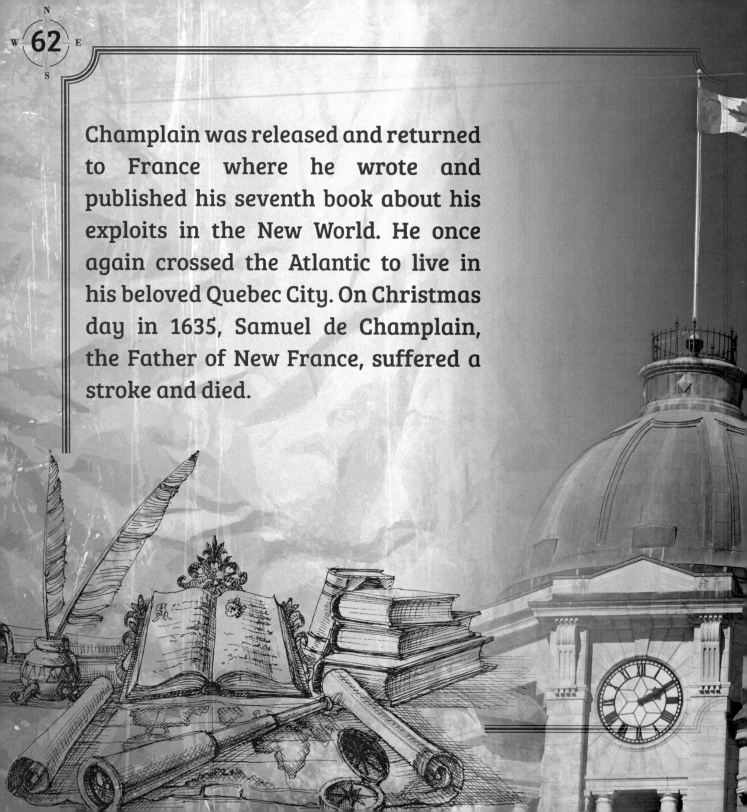

Monument to Samuel De Champlain, founder of the Quebec City with the old Post Office tower in the back, Place D'Armes, Quebec City, Canada

CONCLUSION

Prior to Samuel de Champlain, no European had mapped or explored the region that is now eastern Canada. The thorough and exhaustive expeditions of Champlain led to permanent French settlements in the area that became known as New France. Chief among those settlements was Quebec City, which remains an important center for business and commerce to this day.

Now that you know about the expeditions of Samuel de Champlain, the Father of New France, you are ready to read about other European explorers to the New World.

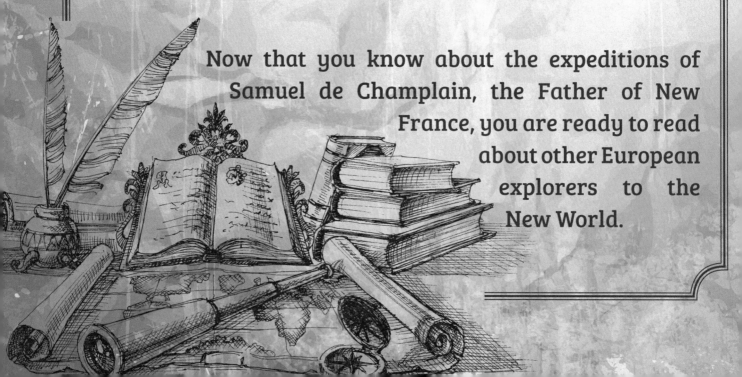

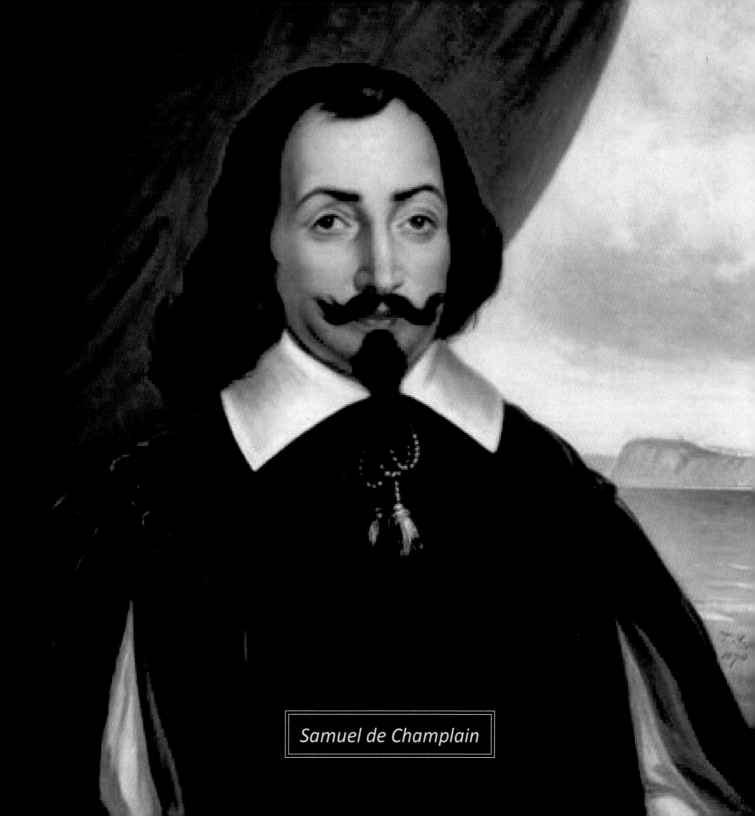

Samuel de Champlain

The old Champlain bridge next to the new Champlain bridge on the Saint Lawrence River seen from the Estacade in Montreal, Quebec, Canada

*Ottawa Canada Landmark
Samuel de Champlain with
Sunset*

Samuel de Champlain at the Habitation at Port-Royal National Historic Site of Canada, Port Royal, Nova Scotia

Visit

www.BabyProfessorBooks.com

to download Free Baby Professor eBooks and
view our catalog of new and exciting Children's
Books